SAFER IN THE PILLOW FORT

SAFER IN THE PILLOW FORT

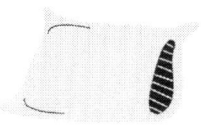

Margaret Claire

Safer In The Pillow Fort

Copyright © 2021 by Margaret Claire
All rights reserved.

ISBN: 978-1-7366891-0-3

Published by Brucher Publishing
www.margaretclaireb.com

"Therefore do not worry about tomorrow, for tomorrow will worry about itself. Each day has enough trouble of its own."

– Matthew 6:34

CONTENTS

I. Unfamiliar

    Heat Lightning During Sunset   3
    Leaving Just To Leave   5
    Missteps Forward   6
    Dirty Water   7
    Stuck In Rewind   8
    Bodies   9
    When The Morning Is Night   10
    Spiraling   12

II. In Winter

    Sleepless   19
    Mirrors On The Wall   21
    Shedding Light   22
    A Cold Sweat   23
    Nocturnal   24
    What Remains   25
    Falling Asleep   26

III. Safer In The Pillow Fort

    Driving Through A Storm   31
    Congenital   33
    Parting Ways   36
    Driving In Circles   37
    In The Center Of Town   38
    Rabbit Hole   39
    Scene Through Cloudy Windows   41

Back In Summer   42
  Falling Asleep II   43

IV. We Are All Changing

  The Kitchen At Three   49
  Early Onset   51
  Homebody   52
  Waiting To Go Home   53
  Purple And Green   55
  Just In Case   57
  The Commute   59
  Wondering, Wandering   61

V. Gently Land

  Soundtrack   67
  Sing Me To Sleep   69
  Everything There Is To Notice   70
  Any Moment Now   72
  A Kiss Goodnight   73
  August Fifteenth   74

  Acknowledgements   77
  About The Author   79

I

Though healthy roots spread,
the ground is unfamiliar.
I used to know you.

Heat Lightning During Sunset

Imagine a strike
    of lightning struck
        across a deceiving sky

in a snapshot,
    a palette knife slashed
        across beautiful canvas

of flowing brushstrokes
    and blended colors,
        fracturing the piece

into tiny fragments,
    splintering glass,
        clouds settling in segments

of geometric
    masterpiece,
        the concept of sky

only surreal
    suggestion. Imagine a
        shattered mirror begging

for a smile
    and blended flesh
        to split into sections,

for eyes to freeze
　　like lightning
　　　　against canvas.

Leaving Just To Leave

While smoke on the inside
of the closed door and shadows
of feet shuffling on the floor flicker
out from underneath, the walls
keep the frequency

of the music from being more
than a ring in her ears,
a bump in her chest;
she's too aware
of her own heartbeat.

Spiraling away
towards the silence of trees
to swish the last of her drink,
she imagines her pillow
burying her head, all sounds

echoing. Her eyelashes
flutter against dirt,
her ceiling
a canopy
of leaves.

Missteps Forward

Each day's partial looking back
    is a track that traces what we once had,
        like fingertips tracing shapes between shoulder blades:
            take a guess, what art am I making?
        The February sun beams hotly
    and heat radiates off the railing at the end
of the path, off of you, there with another,
    my mind in a loop to holding your arm
        and breathing in each other's summer air. Don't look,
    don't look back, but my eyes find a way to loop
through branches and car windshields and eyes
    of others, looking for another down the path
        that keeps curving, that I bend into and walk forward,
    though each step takes me steps back.

Dirty Water

I locked the bathroom door and ran
the sink in a panic, the water running brown
in chunks of muddy jets, flicking
up to hit the foggy mirror. Spots hit
my cheeks and surrounding ceramic.

The water turns to steam
and my skin burns red. The air
is thick, catching in my breath.

I'm digging you out from under my nails
and washing off tainted touches. Like the cracked
tiles under my toes, my palms are stained
with who we were, and I'm craving
the coverage of new hands.

The more I scrub, the more I spill.
My flesh is waterlogged.

Stuck In Rewind

Lost and searching for feeling in your fingertips:

He waits for you knowing, a smoke in hand and a spark

flicking thumb, the safety of old flames, empty kisses

filling lungs, a sip of something to numb impatient,

impartial lips. Each kiss he brings you back

around in circles.

Timing is off; time is cyclical and dull. You chase

counterclockwise with hopes of change, but

he knows you know clocks only tick

one way, and the way you tick he knows

you'll loop back around, like the minute

hand lost amid intoxicating clouds.

Bodies

Lopsided eyes blink
amongst the frayed
rungs of my carpet.

Hair melts and wide
mouths cry down
the tiles of my shower wall.

These faces minus flesh
are unnatural
with twisted noses.

Light flicks
through my curtains
with a wink.

Your presence blends
into these unnamable
faces, like the unrecognizable

shoulders of my coat hangers
and the dead body
of laundry on my floor.

When The Morning Is Night

In the morning
   when the sun
      still hides, it is night.

And I am
   awake, if not
      running away.

And my shoes
   slip and slide and
      sink through the slush.

I am alone
   with icy air
      burning my lungs,

and the only
   road I can take
      is already gone.

So I stop
   to catch
      my breath.

My heart beats,
   but not like it did
      in the summer.

The cold has made
    me warm, but
        my skin chills

to the touch.
    And I have not
        stopped shuddering

ever since you decided you had enough.

Spiraling

This sleeplessness
   is a black hole,
      stretching me thin

so I'm a ray
   by daylight. Told
      to take walks and breaths,

face the depth
   of the blackened sky,
      I sit in the graveyard

in the center
   of town, the quietest
      place I know, the whisperings

coming through
   the roots surely
      my imagination.

On the tracks
   just past the tree
      line, the last train

whizzes by,
   and the plain sky
      has tiny dots

on an infinite canvas
    that do not blink
        or shimmer, their dimness

overwhelming
    my fear of the dark.
        But there's something

like an eyelash
    stuck in the way.
        I wipe my knuckles

over my lids
    and blink until
        the dizzy stars fade.

The smudge still sits
    on the artboard
        sky like spilled ink.

I've read about
    another galaxy
        that we can see

on a clear night
    with the naked eye,
        set on a course to collide

with our Milky Way,
    a cluster of stars
        six billion years away

from meshing
    its identity with ours.
        We will never know

if we deserve it,
    swallowed whole
        by the swollen Sun

turned red giant
    long before it hits.
        Will it happen in a blink?

How can I sleep
    under the sky
        that's not as peaceful as I'm told?

I walk, passing
    tombstones of names
        no longer spoken,

restless still,
    but eased
        by the promise

of nothing. Nothing,
    but also anything, everything,
        the world as we go down with it.

Let us collide,
    let our arms project
        wildly until we settle
            into a new, more beautiful galaxy.

II

*Vulnerable trees
in winter, stripped of their leaves,
still stand (shivering).*

Sleepless

Eyes that close
but keep flipping
back open
because the effort
it takes to weigh
them down when
they are not heavy
is too much
to maintain, though sleep
is calling through
the body, running
up its spine
like a string keeping
it tied to the sheets,
sleep throbbing in
the legs
that are heavy
but also cannot
keep still.

Eyes scan
the walls, the ceiling,
the blinking buttons
on the portable heater
that pushes air
to coat the body,
weighing it down;
eyes blink
at the candles

burning across the room,
dancing in a taunt
to legs that still
cannot fully move
and eyes that still
cannot close,
or when they do,
cannot lock,
because the body
is obsessed with falling
asleep, so self-aware
that it cannot.

Mirrors On The Wall

Behind my eyes I visit my childhood
bedroom and remember my surely
warped full-length mirror. What makes
a home with its reflections?

>There are only three of them
>in our apartment, and they came with it.
>I try not to give my vanity
>its own fragile glass decoration.

I rewind more to standing
on tippy toes to see the rise
of my eyes in the dining room mirror.
>I still sneak peeks of my image

>in picture frames and attempt
>a balancing act on the edge
>of the bathtub. I can't help it.

I slow motion to supper time

and look to my right to acknowledge
my reflection, like it's the only person
I can relate to, as long as it's not midnight.

What is a mirror
>but someone else to run into?

Shedding Light

Her knees clank like chains
during her mid-nightmare,
midnight walk, a visitor
in the halls of her own

house, her body a ghost
floating, light on her toes
and calories, flesh
and bone. Daytime blinded her

with a halo of heaven,
accenting her cheekbones,
kissing her lips. She passes
a black mirror, pausing her joints

as the dark reveals
what it keeps to itself
under the moon and stars,
showing only what exists.

Who is that, with sunken
eyes and a rigid jaw, rolling
their skull off of their spine
and clavicle to look behind

their shoulders, to look
for the skeleton standing
also in the reflection, to find
nobody else, nothing?

A Cold Sweat

Ice kissed gusts of air
shred leaves down the spines
of trees and strip
them to their skeletons,

so they are nothing
but brittle branches
against the charcoal sky.
How can I fall asleep

while the cracking joints
of the splintering tree
scrape against the window,
creep behind the half-open blinds

in a shadow I can't peel
my eyes away from? The cold
from the outside sneaks
into my room. Even under

the weight of my quilt, my eyes
burn from the bitter air
that keeps me awake
and the nightmares that keep me still.

Nocturnal

The nights are quiet spells
that swell stories in my mind,
with the light from the stars
too minimal to relate to.

Even though I know they are vast,
from my sight they are just needles
poking holes through a lid,
until by day it is lifted

and I am blinded by the brightness
projecting from outside.
I can close my eyes and see
bursts of shapes and color

instead of the nothingness
of darkness and dread.

What Remains

The irony of the timing of him coming up again,
as if he started this whole thing at its end.
Why did he lie about where he has been?

But I'm not thoughtful enough; I didn't think to send
a letter, a gift, a gesture of myself to my friend,
as if there's still a piece of me to give. I have always been

a selfish person. No matter how much I pat my skin
dry, I will still spill over with my new, original sin.
A part of us remains where we have been.

Falling Asleep

A sweeping blanket
    is laid out with intention,
        a settling of thought

and shoulders
    and breath, an ease into
        vulnerability and gentle

blinking to fade.
    Yet, despite the
        distinct purpose

to do what we've
    done, we linger
        in fleeting moment,

floating in a sense
    between eyes open
        and close, waiting

for it to arrive —
    but the more we
        ask it to, the more

it waits for us,
    and the more we
        wonder if it ever will.

Falling asleep
    is our wish,
        yet how unsettling

it is when
    unconsciousness
        strikes so suddenly

it seems stolen.
    So suddenly that,
        though we've knowingly

made our bed,
    we do not take a rest.
        It is sleep that takes us.

III

*Quiet and still, we're
safer in the pillow fort
than on winter roads.*

Driving Through A Storm

Keep winter away
with its suffocating quilts,

with its sleet coming down in sheets
on the windshield, tires

slewing through slush, my knuckles white
against the steering wheel

because cars are reckless, roads are crowded
and driving is treacherous in this storm.

Our hearts are cold—but at least still
beating. You sit in the passenger seat

naïve of my desperation to keep
us safe with seatbelt armor and heat

attempting to warm our fingers.
You reach for mine:

But how do I let go of control
to focus on your hand

instead of my nails digging
into the leather of the wheel?

There are no
empty stretches of highway

that weather will not touch,
that others will not rush down,

that go on for miles unscathed
until the gravel reaches a dead end

and a destination
immune to ruin.

Congenital

He keeps three pill bottles,
one in his jacket pocket,
    rattling next to his heart,

one in our kitchen cabinet,
for when we're cooking dinner
and his alarm rings at five-fifty,

one on my bedside table,
just in case he forgets before
    we lay down together,

my head on his chest.
On quiet nights I listen
    to his heartbeat (I don't tell him)
and the way it

    skips
or thumps three times
instead of two,

and I get queasy
because I can hear the force
of the blood swooshing
    in and out, up and down,

heavy and churning—
    like a creek overflowing
in a rainstorm, the water

trying to get past
    a fallen tree, sputtering
up and around the branches
with no clear path, it just has to get there—

but it sounds consistent at least,
it sounds like it's moving,
    like the blood thinner guarantees.

When the heart listening
becomes too much I focus
    on his breathing,
his air like a blanket against my cheek.

On other nights, he sings;
    I lose myself
in his stories and hypotheticals,

forgetting that his lyrics are fiction,
    characters that only exist
between measures and chords.

When it's quiet again, I break
    the spell of alternate realities
through an embrace to focus
    on here and now, a reminder

that our hearts still beat,
    his behind a column of staples.

He is not to blame for my heart twisting,

which is nothing compared to his condition
that he hasn't passed to our daughter—
    never, we think, at least not yet.

Parting Ways

Slipping under
the crack of the door
following the splits
in the wood of the floor
to the opposite side
of our room where we lay,
little noises like ticks
twist with us in the sheets.

Our toes hang off

the edge of our bed

as we stretch

our bodies

thin to escape

the heat and creeks

that keep us awake.

What is it about the night
that sticks
so uncomfortably
to our skin?

Driving In Circles

Even the night sky blanketed

us with oppressive heat, our frayed ends

sticking like splattered paint to our cheeks and our

sheets tangling in the heaps of laundry on the floor.

The shirts draped over the footboard dried

in minutes, like our stiff and cracking lungs.

    We escaped

to my car to find moving air and I carefully

navigated the winding back roads that potholes

spread on, that lend curves we bend into.

You sit in the passenger seat, conscious

of my attempt to distract us from moving. We can

only see as far as the headlights want to show us.

In The Center Of Town

We do not follow the hearse,
but linger in the church,

where the great old branches
of the oak used to hug

the windows. They cut it down
two years ago. Looking through

the panes of the sanctuary,
we see the weary sky, emptiness,

frozen ground and the rotting
stump missing the limbs

that protected it from cold,
like a daughter without her mother,

a husband without his wife.
I never said goodbye

to the tree that occupied
the courtyard of crumbling epitaphs,

carved names not murmured in centuries
indecipherable, with the knuckles

of the oak's roots still
knocking on the tombstones.

Rabbit Hole

I said it could be wasps, can we please go
inside? It was hot and I was afraid
of being stung again. I'm older than you
by a minute, and her by two years,
but you didn't listen, so I stood guard
like a good big sister, watching from across
the yellow yard, the summer heat flicking
off the back of your necks, her hair pouring
out of its ponytail, your sprig of a cowlick
sticking to your forehead, both of you
absorbed with intent, your noses
in the hole in the ground, wondering
who lived down there. It was your idea
to get the garden claw from the garage
we weren't supposed to go in. I should
have said something, but I didn't want to be
the nervous nelly, no fun, tattletale,
big sister, either. I wavered in the distance,
safe in the middle of the yard—away
from the mystery you were sucked into,
afraid of falling, shrinking like Alice,
away from the branches that hung down looming
over your workspace, torn with a twinge
of curiosity that made me wish
I was brave enough to join.

Too stubborn brother with a younger sister
standing too close in adoration, you
and her more twins than the two of us;

you, small for you age and teased for it,
needed momentum to start the great dig.
Throwing weight too heavy, a swing backwards
with the claw went too far and landed
right into her brow. Her shriek shook my knees
into motion: while she ran around the yard
in circles, her hands gripping the top of her head,
I ran inside to get mom. All it needed
was peroxide, so she sat on the counter
in tears, mom playing nurse, dad yelling,
you crying that it was an accident,
the wasp nest open in the front yard, angry,
swarming with stingers.

Scene Through Cloudy Windows

I drove to your house through Emmaus early
while snow, a swelling moment in the air,
ached on the branches. On each side of the road
that guided me in a drift along the tracks
of cars passed, sliding in tow with traffic
(only pumping the brakes for the illusion
of control), houses I've never seen over
and over again suddenly shown against
the stark white of fresh snow. My eyes
moved from their urgent focus on blurry
taillights ahead to instead follow the motion
of the windshield wipers, then to trace the brick
constructions around stone façades
and stained-glass front doors; skipping
from each mailbox to driveway end,
from buried cars to more homes winding
along the street, curving through backroads
that my sight couldn't reach. I imagined lives,
moments of family: children home
from school early rolling in snow, animals
in a leap chasing snowballs and parents
shoveling the storm to curb and retreating
to fire crackling in orange glow
through the window.

                      Oh, if I make it back
let's play and build a makeshift igloo home.

Back In Summer

Remember the drunken pulse in the air,
the heaviness of summer heat
but the weightlessness of the chills
running up our arms?

Remember the breath of oak stirring
the night with desire, the atmosphere
a blanket wrapping around our
shoulders, a breeze whispering temptations
maybe we would refuse come winter?

Remember: when winter kicks in again
and the air's veins freeze over — the nights
stretching into the days and the wind
in thrashing sleepwalk —

remember
to let us sway in slow dance,
allowing the heat of our bodies to guide us
through the stillness of snow.

Falling Asleep II

A humble posture
    is taken with purpose,
        an acknowledgement

of presence,
    a settling of thought
        and shoulders and breath,

praise and
    confession. But
        my words linger

on what I've
    done, and my lips
        mouth with lessening

connection,
    unconscious
        repetition.

Sleep ...
    so intoxicating ...
        My thoughts run

in circles
    and all sense
        is missing.

Maybe if
　　I catch myself
　　　　I can get back

on track,
　　but then
　　　　I'm awake,

hours passed
　　and a prayer
　　　　never finished.

You gift me rest,
　　even though I
　　　　don't deserve it.

IV

The summer sun shines,
yet leaves crunch beneath our feet.
We are all changing.

The Kitchen At Three

You pull   on the refrigerator door
        and it   pulls back too,
rattling the bottles in the shelf

until the   pressure
releases with an exhale   of cool air
and leftovers skim under your nose,

only for you to swing it shut again
        with a sigh,
because   you cannot find
what you are looking for,
        and the light-bulb shines

too bright for this blurry hour
        of not yet morning, not quite night.
        As you   gaze
at the closed metallic door, a slight

wobble
        in your knees, dizzy eyes, and tilt
in your head, there is a flicker
of wonder if that light
        ever actually turns off,

which soon evolves into a fixation,
        like hoping that when the sky is clouded,
        the stars still   exist.

So you squint   into the crack of the door,
your eyelashes touching the edge,
> moving,
> closing,
> slowly inching,

and just before the magnetic strips   touch
there is a click, a recognition—
> the light switches
> off.

And while you find satisfaction

in the finality of bearing witness
> to this great mystery,

you are also disappointed
> that it is   over, and you   wonder

if the stars are still alive
> when they are behind the clouds
> and not shining,

even though you know   they are not.

Early Onset

I remember when you sewed
the quilt I drape around your shaking
shoulders. Winter has kicked in,
though your mind is back in summer.

The design you artfully patched clings
to your body, with the mess of stitches
and knots hidden inside the seams.
You do not share your visions

anymore. The edges are beginning
to fray, threadbare, folded
over and over; like your memories,
we cannot see its beauty.

You were never good at talking
with a stranger. So, we sit
in silence, shivering with tea.
I do not recognize you, either.

Homebody

Resting somewhere new
to me is the same unfamiliar
feeling of flying in a plane.
Are we meant to?

I could be blanketed
warm or buckled in,
my feet could touch the ground
or what's left of it,

but I will still feel
that weightlessness
in the pit of my stomach.
It's like lifting off and settling

at altitude. We are safe
until we are not. Away from
home is where we are
and where my heart is not.

Waiting To Go Home

Eyes locked
in a stare across
the fluorescents;
eyes unblinking,
sunken in dizzy
head, straining to lift
from the pillow,
hair like whispers
clinging to the sheet.
Eyes fixed
on the corner,
a blurry longing
for who's not really there,
not there at all.
Eyes cloudy
in memory
staring at cinderblock
and rewinding;
eyes gazing past
lashes,
clinical curtains
and unknown faces;
eyes seeing nothing
but imagination.

Neck craning up
and up, the apparition
dissolving
back to summer;

eyes avoiding
the others.

Ears listening
to buzzing honeybee;
lips slurring
incoherently.

Purple And Green

The clouds threaten
to swallow your backyard
whole, the empty swings
whipping around the monkey bars
by the wind, the shrieking
air less like a train, more
like ghosts on the playset
showing off how high
they can go, but nobody
is looking, as if closing
the curtains can hide
you from your neighbors
and erase the brewing storm,
as if changing the channel
from the weather report
can make the weather go away—
but storm systems form
with no regard to the structure
of your home.

Locking yourself in your room
can't keep the bullet-
like rain from barreling
against the shingles,
or the water from pooling
under the gap of your door,
or the slams and shouts
in the living room from rattling
your dresser. Purple and green

clouds twist to the ground
like your upper arms
after a few days of healing,
physically, at least,
because you can't clean
the destruction of a tornado
until the clouds recede.

Just In Case

I keep the eight pills
I have left in the secret
    slot of my bag,

just in case I get
nervous enough. But they go bad
    in April, meant

for the trip I never
took. But knowing they're there
    is a relief,

so much so that
I haven't had to take
    one, at least not yet.

I keep a journal
not even a quarter used
    at my bedside,

just in case I have
an idea worth saving
    in permanence,

or a dream that I need
to remember, it might tell
    me something important,

but if it's that
important, I'm sure I'll
    remember it in the morning.

These things I do not
open. Maybe
    it's the commitment

of losing my
backup plan, or a perfectly
    clean notebook.

The Commute

I look through my windshield, like the shards
of headlight glass scattered on gravel
look up to face the blue cloud speckled
sky, as if something like colliding hard

could happen on a sunny day, any other day,
like the driver stumbling out from the wreckage
to collapse on the road, limbs in all directions,
so he can look up and maybe pray, his eyes fixed

on the sun in the same way I'm fixed on him
now. The accident made us divert our paths
into the parking lot, and as we pass
our heads turn to see what happened, how,

was everyone okay, and could the same
thing happen to us? We inch through
the lot, eyes darting from windshield to rear view
to left window, every car in line the way we came

like a procession, a kaleidoscope image
of heads turning, cars crawling, eyes
shifting, heads turning, enough times
to strain our necks, as we pass the finish

line and brake before we hit
the car in front of us, everyone trying to see
what might have happened in reality
as we drive away from it.

And the next day, my eyes will follow
the yellow line, looking for signs
of yesterday in the littered shine
of glass, only winks of hollow

light to suggest it might have happened,
but there are no major signs,
only memory and glass swept to the side
so we can all continue in our direction.

Wondering, Wandering

On the tracks just past
    the tree line, the train makes
        its rounds in entropic clockwork,

its desperate whistle
    in tantrum so it can't
        be missed, a crescendo of rattling

rails, shifting cargo —
    and it's a wonder why
        the wheels don't slip off the line

as it begs to pass.
    I almost expect
        it to take flight.

My bedroom walls
    tremble as the night train
        hurries by. Sometimes

the cry of the whistle
    sounds louder, more
        urgent than other times,

the procession
    lurching forward.
        I can't place this

sense of dread.
    I imagine the railcars
        blending together

in between branches
    so the train appears
        in rumbling slow motion,

even though it can't
    be stopped. And I can't
        help but remember

the headlines of someone's
    waiting, wandering along
        the tracks, the train's

attempt to stop too late.
    Or maybe you were
        just playing a game,

hovering there
    with your ear low,
        your arms splayed across

the ties, listening
    for the hiss of the rails
        to predict the next train's

arrival — yes, a game.
    Waiting, wondering,
        wandering. My bedroom walls

settle as the night
    train disappears.
        Where are we going?

V

*Honeybee suspends
itself mid-air, deciding
where to gently land.*

Soundtrack

Splayed on the floor,
ears pressed into the cut
pile carpet, the wooly
texture not muffling
sound like expected,
instead it's like holding
an ear to a shell,
can you hear
the ocean's secrets?

Your pages pulling,
a swift but drawn-out
flick as you catch
the last word
and anticipate the next;
the train approaching,
a soft and distant
thunder, the ground
a resonant purr
against my temple;
the voices
of our neighbors
downstairs drowned out
by each other besides
the distinct sing-along
of happy birthday.

The train doesn't shriek
as it approaches,

no, it harmonizes.

Sing Me To Sleep

For a while we have stayed inside,
the closed door and shadows
our friends, though we can hear
our neighbors shuffling. The walls
dampen your music

from across the apartment,
but the buzz of your guitar
still strings down the hall
like static electricity.

I can't hear what you sing
but I can feel the thump
of the heel of your palm
on your acoustic,
your intonation slipping
under the crack of the door,
seeking me from eternity.

I can't hear it but I can
taste it, sweet like honey
coating my throat,
in the pressure
of my head
and sinuses,
your melody.

Everything There Is To Notice

I.
When you go up one-hundred, turn left
and make another, drive under the same
swaying traffic lights and curves I bend
into, pass by the two bakeries I've never
tried, notice the continuous construction
around the bridge on Chestnut, the workers
directing traffic, the Baptist church's daily-
changing sign, faces in opposing windshields
talking or texting or indifferent, except
the bus driver who laughed. Wonder, to who?

II.
Do you see the poems in my commute?
I see them, too: They dwell in my mind until
they're ripe enough to write down.
Like when the car that crashed on Tuesday
made us divert our paths into the strip mall's
lot, but on Wednesday we kept going the same
daily way, though the pavement felt different,
as if the shards of window glass asked me to tell
you about that moment (so I will). Fleeting
moments are not so fleeting in my head.

III.
Then quarantine hit and the poems untangled
themselves from my brain, fading, the monotonous
commute of intricately crafted lives passing by,
no more. Now blink and six months or more
have gone by. I don't see any construction workers,

just the tractor's arm reaching into the sky,
and the bus driver's laugh or frown or indifference
hidden under her mask.

But at least the church's sign still changes,
maybe now more people will notice.

Any Moment Now

We try to control what comes next. But in an instant
He will come back, when we are too focused
on what could happen next. Let's take one moment

at a time. A slow contentment, as every second
passes I will recognize the ways I am broken
and be grateful for it. Let's take every moment

for what it is: a gift. A release from the past, minute
by minute we get closer to it. Until then, my soul is chosen.
Who is your heart at any moment?

A Kiss Goodnight

My mind lingers in the church,
on the Presbyterian minister's

words. This was before I understood,
but it has stuck with me ever since

I visited the pews of the sanctuary
four years ago. Even though our puffy coats

crammed us beside each other,
it was the first time I could sit there

without suffocating, besides
the suffocation from the knot

knocking on my throat. But
that's a different story. He spoke

of a love story, the foundation
of an oak tree, its stump

like a rock. Cut off for now
but it is steadfast,

like the love of the Father and Son,
a husband with his bride.

It was a story of eternity
that ended with a kiss goodnight.

August Fifteenth

I let my fear
   cloud around you
      to hide you from

my mindset,
   as if my poetry
      had to be external

targets, not too
   close to home.
      But then there are moments

like today
   at the altar,
      and I see your poetry.

Not the fear
   I have relating
      to you, but the little

things there are to notice.

I could write
   about you forever.
      In fact, I vow to.

Acknowledgements

An effort of five-plus years, writing this collection of poetry was as much of a journey as I hope it is to you reading it. It started in a flash fiction writing class at college and paused during a string of hiatuses as I explored (or stubbornly ignored) my creative outlets. But, here it is—and I have many to thank for it finally coming alive.

First, I have to start by thanking God. I did not know You when I first started writing, but You were with me and blessed me along my path. Thank You for drawing me near to You and for Your love and grace.

To Alan-Michael: My husband, my muse, my beta reader, and love of my life and beyond. Thank you for your encouragement, patience, and love. For your spiritual leadership and creative brainstorming sessions. For taking the lead on "house stuff" while I heads-down write. For reminding me to take breaks, take care of myself, and pray. I love you.

To my parents: Thank you for motivating me to "make it happen." For supporting my creative ventures and times of purple hair. I finally published that "novel" you thought I was working on all these years. Thank you for your patience as it took me a while to muster up the courage to share.

To Bob Watts, Associate Professor of English at Lehigh University: Thank you for your hand in editing many of the poems in this collection. Thank you for influencing my passion for poetry and introducing me to other poets who have shaped my craft.

And thank you to all of my friends, family, and readers who have encouraged me and read my poetry along the way.

About The Author

Margaret Claire is a writer, poet, and marketing professional whose creative ventures fall second to her passion for God. She lives in Eastern Pennsylvania with her husband Alan-Michael and their beloved cat Charlie.

Visit Margaret Claire's website to sign up for her mailing list and get more content and updates:

margaretclaireb.com

Printed in Great Britain
by Amazon